Morgan and the Bear

Based On a True Story

Morgan and the Bear

Based On a True Story

Mona Gilbert Ball, as told to
Angela Kelsey

Illustrations by
Joseph and Steven Baum

Published by Madison Avenue Press
www.MadisonAvenuePress.com
an imprint of
Madison Avenue Publishing, Inc.
275 Madison Avenue
14th Floor
New York, NY 10016
www.MadisonAvenuePublishing.net

Ball, Mona Gilbert
Morgan and the Bear-Based On a True Story
As told to Angela Kelsey
Illustrations by Joseph and Steven Baum
p.cm

1. Ball, Mona Gilbert 2. Ball, Mona Gilbert-family. 3. Ball, Mona
Gilbert-father. 4. Florida-pioneers-Estero Island. 5. Florida-pioneers-
boyhood-coming of age. 6. Florida-children living in rural areas.
7.Florida-history-biography. 8. Florida-wild animals. I. Title
F319.E8.B35 2011
975.94806bal

Library of Congress Control Number: 2011940908

ISBN 978-1-937757-00-7

Dedicated to My Great-Grandchildren
Robert Burton Black
and
Sydney Elizabeth Black

~

In Honor of My Father
Morgan Albert Gilbert

It was early morning.

I was still asleep when the roar of a bear woke me up.

He was close to our house and, from the sound of his voice, he was a monster.

"Mamma, I'm gonna get that bear," I said at breakfast.

My mother flipped hoecakes for my little brother, Will, and me in her big iron skillet.

She was quiet, and I knew she didn't want me to go.

Later, I told her I wanted to track and kill the bear because it would probably come back.

"I can be the man of the house," I said.

Daddy had taken a trip to Myers to deliver our tomatoes and meet with the City Commission.

She finally agreed.

She said I could go for one night, and then, whether I caught the bear or not, I had to come home.

She packed some biscuits, leftover fried chicken, and some vegetables for our trip to track the bear.

We picked tomatoes in the morning and did other chores.

Finally we were off.

I knew we would get that bear.

Will and I made our plans.

I carried Daddy's shotgun and
Will carried our bag of food.

We stopped by our favorite fishing hole on the other side of the island.

Our fishing poles were in the secret hiding place, just where we'd left them.

We fished for a couple of hours, but we didn't catch anything.

We would get the bear, though.

That was what was important.

As we walked along, looking for tracks, the island became like a jungle, with mangroves, palmettos, and all kinds of prickly bushes.

We saw our first bear tracks, and some panther tracks, too, but no bears were anywhere to be seen.

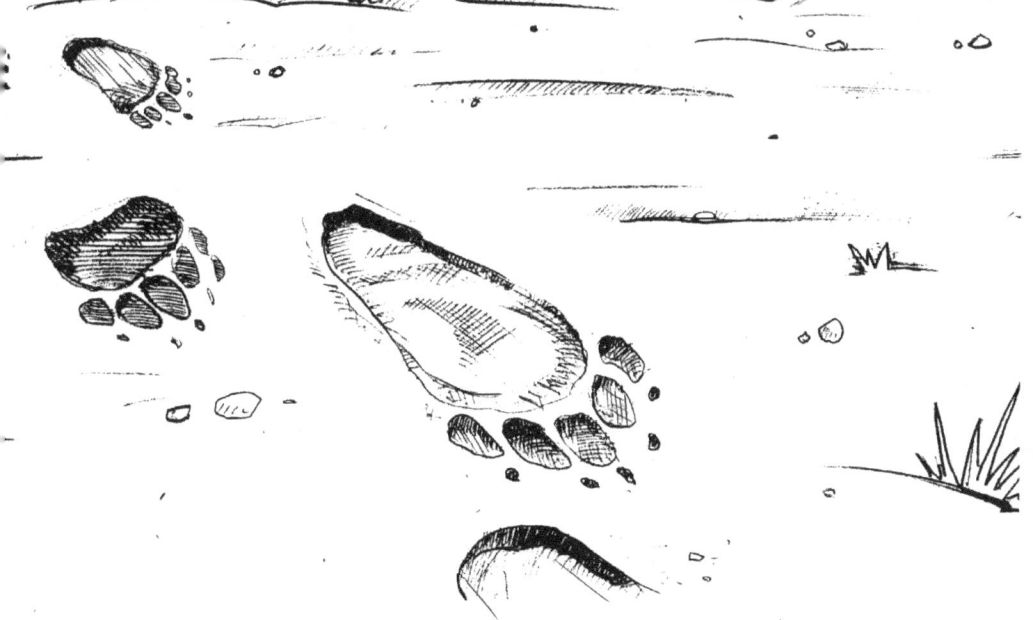

Late in the day when it was still light we made a campfire. As the sun set it was a little scary. "What if the bear sees our fire?" my brother asked. "I have Daddy's shotgun," I said. "Don't worry."

Just before it became really dark, but after our fire had almost gone out, we heard a noise in the bushes nearby. "Did you hear that?" my little brother said. I nodded. "I'll bet it's that big bear. Let's go get him," I said as I picked up Daddy's shotgun.

We bent over and walked in the direction the noise had come from. The bushes were thick, but we saw some big bear tracks. We could hear the sound of something stepping on bushes ahead of us. "We're getting close," I said.

As soon as we walked out of the
underbrush, there he was!

He reared up and let out a roar that shook my insides. He must have weighed five hundred pounds!

I got off one shot that must have hit him, but the shotgun jammed when I tried to shoot again.

Will was already running when I turned and followed him. I ran for my life!

The enormous creature caught up with me, slapped me with his huge paw, and knocked me ten feet into the air.

My shotgun landed in the other direction.

I tried to get my gun, but I couldn't reach it.

I tried to get my knife out of my pocket, but then, just as I thought that bear was going to eat me alive, he ran away.

Will came over to see if I was still breathing.

"I'm okay. But it's too late to track him tonight," I said.

We walked back to our camp.

The next morning we went back to where the bear had chased me.

We walked up a creek and saw the bear's huge paw prints in the mud.

"I think he is limping," I said.

Will thought that he had covered his wounds in mud.

We followed his tracks deeper into the mangrove forest.

Just when we thought we would not find him again, there he was!

He limped, but he let out a roar again that scared me.

I told Will to hurry and climb a tree.

The giant bear came closer to me and stood up on his hind legs.

He looked like he was seven feet tall!

I fired two more shots.

Captain Kindall, a local boat captain, and one other man showed up with another rifle.

My neighbors on the island celebrated the big event with a big feast in our honor.

Everyone brought a plate of food to share.

When Daddy got home from Myers, we had a family dinner, and I told him all about our adventure in the woods.

He said I really had been the man of the house while he was away.

Fort Myers News-Press Nov. 30, 1897

Estero Island News

I thought I would, with your permission, drop you a few lines to tell you about this beautiful little island, its possibilities, sport etc. I wish you could be with us for a while and see the many things that are pleasing to the eye.

Had you been with us on the 15th inst., you might have had some rare sport. Morgan A. Gilbert went hunting, yes hunting for bear and he found three, the third and last one he shot at was a very large one, weighting about 500 pounds. He crept up to within 50 or 60 feet of the bear before being scented and as the bear raised up on his hind feet and looked at him, Morgan fired one charge into Mr. Bruin, which only enraged him and with an unearthly yell he charged Morgan. Of course the other barrel failed to fire, then Morgan felt for his hunting knife, but by this time the bear was upon him and came with such force that he knocked Morgan about ten feet one way and the gun the other. Think what a place to be put in, over in the sand on your back expecting every second a large, ferocious brute to tear you to pieces. But to his astonishment, on arising, the brute was going at a great rate through briars, etc. into the jungle, a very

Morgan Albert Gilbert
Photo courtesy of F. D. Gilbert

dense hammock. That being about 9 o'clock at night, and not having a dog the chase had to be abandoned till daylight, when the trail was taken up and followed with great ease until it came to water, when it was found that the bear had plugged up his wounds with mud, and with difficulty the trail was followed three-fourths of a mile further, often on hands and knees, in the palmettos. In this position, to his surprise, he found himself face to face with the bear, standing on the defense and growling defiance at a distance of about five feet, and to make matters worse Morgan had his little brother, a lad about 8 years, with him. Hurriedly he bade the lad to climb a small tree at hand, before the battle should commence with bruin standing ground defying him all the time. The next thing was to be sure of his aim as he had only had one load of buck-shot and one load of No.2 shot left, so he took good aim and pulled the trigger again, and down tumbled Mr. Bruin; then the charge of No.2 shot was fired at such close rang that the wad was driven into the bear, and still he was not dead, but showed fight, with one fore leg and one hind leg broken. About this time, however, Mrs. Gilbert sent Morgan a Marlin rifle by Capt. Kindall and bear was soon dispatched. The next question was how shall we get the meat home but about this time Robt. King, who had heard the shooting, came up, and rendered valuable assistance in skinning, cutting up the meat and carrying it home. I never saw a fatter animal. The fat on the hams being an inch thick, and the hide was very pretty.

I think it must have been the hand of God that saved Morgan, for he never received a scratch, although he was, as he says, knocked about ten feet and his gun the other way.

On the 16th Mr. Jessie Graham was hunting for possums in his tomato patch and ran across another bear which the dog treed and Jessie shot at it twice with a revolver without hitting anything. However the shots brought Mr. Smith and Robt. King to the to the scene and after a short chase bruin was laid low.

Yes we are having lots of fun and getting some fine meat. Come down and we will try to give you a pleasant time. Fishing is good as well as hunting. Crops look fine and are doing well, and although, it has been very dry for some time we can't say that tomatoes are suffering for rain.

I hope this won't find its very way to the waste basket..... You never saw a broader smile on an elephant's face than on Jessie's face after the bear he killed, and as for Morgan, well we can't describe his feelings that he had killed a fine bear, and all the while his father was in Myers. **Burton.**

www.ingramcontent.com/pod-product-compliance
Lightning Source LLC
Chambersburg PA
CBHW031529040426
42445CB00009B/455